Canine SARTECH™ Workbook

Designed as a preparatory guide for canine teams planning to take the NASAR Canine SARTECH™ certification examination

First Printing 2000
First Revision June 2005

Table of Contents

Introduction

In 2000, the National Association for Search and Rescue (NASAR) SAR Dog Section under the direction of Cheryl Kennedy, Section Chairperson, organized the development of a workbook. This workbook was designed to benefit the canine community by helping them prepare for the required written test associated with the NASAR Canine SARTECH™ certification program.

To move things forward, the project was assigned to Regional Representatives as part of their duties. As the project progressed, several individuals were asked to assist in proofreading and writing certain sections. It was a collaborative effort by all involved to produce a document that would be of benefit to the entire canine community.

NASAR would like to recognize the following people who spent countless hours in writing, proofreading, and assisting in the grammaticism of the original workbook:

- **Cheryl Kennedy** - NASAR Canine Section Chairperson; Larimer County Search and Rescue/Colorado Search and Rescue Dogs of Colorado, Ft. Collins, Colorado

- **Dee Wild** – NASAR Canine Section Regional Representative, Region VI; Louisiana Search and Rescue Dog Team, Lacombe, Louisiana

- **Julie L.S. Weibler** – Larimer County Search and Rescue; Colorado Search and Rescue Dogs of Colorado, Severence, Colorado

- **Lisa Higgins** – Louisiana Search and Rescue Dog Team, Pearl River, Louisiana

- **Philip Kuper** – Louisiana Search and Rescue Dog Team, Slidell, Louisiana

***

First Revision June 2005 by NASAR SAR Dog Section Committee

Workbook Description

The Canine SARTECH™ workbook was developed as an informal guide to introduce the fundamentals of canine handling. There is no formal NASAR course associated with this level of certification. However, this guide demonstrates how the user can combine both classroom and practical application to prepare for the Canine SARTECH™ Certification exam. For our purposes, we will call it a "review" rather than a "course."

Recommended Schedule

The Canine SARTECH™ review will generally consist of 20 hours.

Workbook Objectives

- To provide canine handlers with a review of the fundamentals of canine search and rescue operations.
- To prepare canine handlers to successfully complete the Canine SARTECH™ Certification examination.

Knowledge, Skills and Abilities

The testing candidate should be prepared to demonstrate an understanding of the following:

1. Canine obedience
2. Canine health, agility and fitness
3. Expectations of working canine
4. Canine first aid
5. Canine handler responsibilities/expectations
6. Legal aspects of training and search work
7. Scent theory
8. Knowledge of the following disciplines:
    a. Tracking/Trailing
    b. Airscent
    c. Human Remains Detection
    d. Avalanche
    e. Disaster
    f. Evidence/Article search
9. Directionals
10. Canine alerts and refinds
11. Helicopter/Aircraft operations with a canine
12. Rappelling with a canine
13. Canine equipment
14. Handler equipment
15. Search techniques and tactics
16. Interfacing support team and canine team
17. Terminology

Testing Requirements

1. Candidate must have successfully completed NASAR SARTECH™ II (non-canine)*
2. Candidate must show written proof of the canine having successfully completed a nationally recognized obedience evaluation, which meets or exceeds the American Kennel Club's Canine Good Citizen test.
3. Candidate must possess all of the equipment as listed in NASAR's Canine SARTECH™ Certification Program Area Search and Tracking/Trailing/Land Personal and Canine First Aid and Survival Kit, also known as the "24-Hour Pack for Canine Handlers". This list is available on the NASAR website at www.nasar.org.

*Some dog owners mistakenly believe that only the canine requires training to become a valuable SAR resource. NASAR's fundamental philosophy is that the canine is a SAR tool. In order to effectively conduct a search mission, it is critical that the handler be well qualified as a SAR responder before attempting to become certified as a canine handler.

Note on Certification with Multiple Canines
The Canine SARTECH™ Certification is only valid for the specific canine handler team evaluated. Other canines trained by the same handler must undergo the entire evaluation process separately.

Lesson One

This lesson is intended to help the candidate better understand how to respond to canine health issues, and how to assess and treat injuries and illnesses which could occur during a search or training exercise.

A SAR dog handler should be able to recognize a potential canine health problem, understand how to treat the injury/illness, know the canine's normal and abnormal vital signs, and understand canine nutrition and fitness. With this knowledge, the candidate will be able to better sustain his or her canine partner's health and well-being. It should be noted that this lesson only briefly discusses some of the numerous health issues that could affect a canine in the field. The handler is strongly urged to seek additional knowledge through courses taught by veterinarians or books specifically written on canine first aid.

I. General Health of the Working Canine

Nutrition

A working canine needs a balanced diet along with exercise in order to perform at the highest degree of mental and physical capability. It is vital to the health and well-being of the canine to have the essential nutrients and vitamins, which promote stamina and endurance, found in quality canine foods. During long searches, the canine's body will rely on these factors to keep it going.

It is also recommended that special canine endurance products, along with plenty of fresh water, be made available to the canine during long searches. A canine should be monitored for factors, such as dehydration, affecting its work,.

Physical Fitness

In order to develop a canine's working stamina, it is important that daily exercise be included as part of training. It should not be expected that a canine receiving very little exercise will be able to work for long periods of time in the field. A working canine is very similar to a human athlete. The athlete maintains a diet specifically geared to improve his stamina and endurance combined with stretching exercises before going out to compete. The canine should be provided the same considerations.

II. Assessment of a Canine

It is suggested that a candidate take the time to learn the canine's normal vital signs during rest as well as after a workout. This will better assist the candidate in determining when the canine's vital signs are not within a safe limit. The normal vital sign ranges are:

> *Heart Rate – 80 to 120 beats per minute*
> *Respirations – 12 to 30 per minute*
> *Rectal Temperature – 101 to 102.5 degrees*
> *Capillary Refill Time – less than 2 seconds*

- <u>To check a canine's heart rate</u>, place fingertips or palm against the left side of the canine's chest just behind the elbow. Count the number of beats for 15 seconds and multiply that number by 4 to get the number of beats per minute.

- <u>To check the canine's pulse</u>, place the fingertips gently on the femoral artery located on the inside of the thigh where the leg joins the body. Feel for the quality of the pulse to determine if it is thready and weak, steady and strong, or bounding and hard.

- <u>To check the canine's capillary refill time</u>, quickly press under the canine's upper lip (mucous membrane) with a fingertip to see how long it takes for the lip to go from white to pink. It should take no more than 2 seconds to refill.

Assessing a Canine for Life-threatening Injuries
The initial assessment of a canine is to identify a life-threatening injury by implementing the ABC's - Airway (A), Breathing (B) and Circulation (C).

- Airway – Is the canine's airway blocked causing difficulty in breathing or lack of breathing? To open an airway line up the tongue in the mouth and extend the head and neck. Check inside the mouth and clear any debris or foreign materials with a sweep of your finger.

- Breathing – Observe for breathing for ten seconds. Make sure the chest rises and falls and air can be felt moving in and out of the dog's mouth or nose.

- Circulation – Check for a heartbeat - put your hand on the sternum or place your hand on the chest. Check the femoral pulse.

Performing CPR on a Canine
First check the breathing. Pull the tongue forward and wipe out any excess saliva or vomit (clear the airway). If breathing is not observed, begin artificial respiration. To perform mouth-to-mouth or mouth-to-nose respiration, pull the canine's tongue forward over the lower teeth. Hold the canine's mouth shut—trapping the tongue will keep it from obstructing the airway. Cover the canine's nose with your mouth and force air into the canine's nostrils. As the air is forced into the nostrils, look for the canine's chest to rise. Take your mouth off the canine's nose and allow the air to flow out of the lungs. Give two to four full breaths at a rate of 25 to 30 times per minute, and then recheck the canine's pulse and heartbeat. If no pulse or heartbeat is detected, begin chest compressions. In medium to large breeds, compress the chest wall using two hands. Place canine on its right side on a firm surface, place your hands over the heart on the left side of his chest and begin compressions. Do 5 chest compressions for every breath with a rate of 80 to 120 times per minute.

Secondary Assessment
After determining the ABCs, a secondary survey should be performed. Examine the canine from head to tail. Use a methodical approach in order to check the entire canine. It is recommended that the candidate survey the canine partner on a regular basis. This will help

the candidate develop a pattern for conducting the survey as well as assisting in detecting injuries.

III. Use of Human Medications for Canines

There are times when it is easier to administer human medication to a canine because of availability. It is important to know whether or not the more common human medications are safe for canine use. Although this section will discuss a few medications, the candidate is encouraged to talk with his veterinarian to see what other human medications may be safely used.

- Buffered aspirin – 5 milligrams per 1 pound (weight of canine) every 12 hours for pain relief or as an anti-inflammatory.

- Benadryl (an antihistamine) – 1 milligram per 1 pound (weight of canine) every 12 hours. It is widely used for allergic reactions to insect bites such as bee stings.

- Motrin/Advil (ibuprofen) – Not recommended for canine use.

- Pepto Bismol (bismuth subsalicylate) – 1 tablespoon per 15 pounds (weight of canine) every 6 hours for vomiting and diarrhea.

- Tylenol (acetaminophen) – Not recommended for canine use.

IV. Handling Various Canine Injuries

Brief descriptions of some common canine afflictions and injuries, including symptoms and treatments, are listed below.

- **Arthritis** – Typically affects larger breeds. Obesity can aggravate the condition. The symptoms include pain, lameness and stiffness of the joints. Pain relievers, moderate activity, warm/dry environments help keep the joints from stiffening.

- **Bicipital Tenosynovitis** – Inflammation of the biceps brachii tendon and the surrounding synovial sheath from direct or indirect trauma, repetitive injury or overuse. This results in intermittent or progressive forelimb lameness that worsens after exercise. The condition usually presents as a forelimb lameness, showing pain upon flexion of the elbow and direct palpation of the biceps tendon. Treatment involves rest and a non-steroidal anti-inflammatory drug (NSAID) such as aspirin.

- **Bloat** – Typically occurs when a canine eats a big meal, drink lots of water and then exercises within two to three hours after eating. The stomach fills with gas and/or fluids, swells, and may become twisted. Bloat is a very serious, life-threatening situation that could cause death if not treated by a veterinarian. Handlers should be aware of this possibility, as it is never known when the canine will be pressed into action. The signs and symptoms include extreme restlessness, salivation, drooling, and dry heaves. The abdomen will be distended and the canine may go into shock.

Immediate intervention to decompress and reposition the stomach provides the best chance for survival.

- **Cranial Cruciate Ligament Injury** – Typically occurs when the cranial cruciate ligament, which is located in the knee joint, tears abruptly during exercise. The signs and symptoms include sudden limping and pain. This injury requires surgery to repair.

- **Dehydration** – Decrease in total body water to less than normal. The signs include sunken eyes, dry mucus membranes and slow capillary refill time. To treat, provide canine with water, small amounts at a time.

- **Dysplasia** – Faulty development of the hip or elbow joint characterized by degrees of joint shallowness and laxity that permit subluxation (slipping out of place). As the condition progresses, deformation of the acetabulum and femoral head is accompanied by the development of degenerative joint disease (arthritis). The condition presents as a lameness and/or irregular gait such as "bunny hopping" in the rear. Other similar anatomical growth abnormalities affect the shoulders, elbows, stifles, and hocks. These types of lamenesses are treated with rest and anti-inflammatories. If signs do not improve with rest and anti-inflammatories, referral to a veterinarian for radiographs and further treatment is recommended.

- **Fracture** – Typically occurs as a result of a trauma, and is classified as either open or closed. An open fracture is more serious since the end of the bone breaks through the skin, causing tissue damage and possibly promoting infection. The signs can include disfigurement and/or an open wound with bone exposed. To treat, use splints to restrict movement of the affected area. Transport canine to a veterinarian. If bone fragments or the end of the bone can be seen, place a clean bandage over the area to help prevent contamination.

- **Frostbite** – Occurs following exposure to a cold environment with body temperatures dropping below 93 degrees Fahrenheit; following freezing of any exposed body surface; or contact with cold liquid, glass or metal. Most commonly affected areas are the ears, tail, external genitalia and footpads. Signs include pale skin that is cool to the touch, due to decreased circulation in the affected area. As the area(s) are thawed, the canine will experience pain and localized swelling. The area(s) should be slowly thawed out. Do not rub a frozen area as tissues are easily bruised or torn. If at all possible, bring the canine into a warm shelter, cover with a blanket or other material.

- **Heat Exhaustion** – Typically occurs when the canine is left inside a closed car or poorly ventilated area on a hot day or when over-worked during hot weather. The canine will experience fast, shallow breathing and rapid heartbeat. Body temperature will be elevated, and the canine may go into shock. Immediately sponge the canine with cool water and seek veterinary care at immediately.

- **Heat Stroke** – Occurs from exposure to excessive heat without adequate ventilation or cooling mechanisms in place. The signs and symptoms include elevated body temperature (over 103 degrees Fahrenheit), seizures, depression, coma and congested mucous membranes. Begin oxygen administration, cool the body down by rinsing or sponging with cool water--concentrate on the neck over the jugular veins and the abdomen. Do not immerse! Monitor the body temperature, and stop rinsing the body with cool water when the temperature reaches 103.0 – 103.5 degrees Fahrenheit in order to avoid hypothermia. Seek veterinary attention immediately.

- **Hypothermia** – Occurs from exposure to a cold environment with inadequate shelter. When the rectal temperature drops below 82 degrees Fahrenheit the canine will lose the ability to return its body temperature to normal. Canine hypothermia should be treated as aggressively as human hypothermia. The signs and symptoms are similar to those humans experience. Place the canine in a warm setting and wrap with warm blankets; apply warm water bottles using a towel or blanket between the bottle and the canine's skin to avoid thermal burns; or immerse in warm water. It is important to slowly bring up the canine's core body temperature.

- **Shock** – Typically occurs after a major trauma that affects circulation. The signs and symptoms include lethargy, labored breathing, pale gums and elevated heart rate. The canine becomes weak and depressed; pupils may be dilated; pulse is weak and rapid; capillary refill is slow to occur. If the canine has suffered a bleeding wound, apply pressure to the wound and keep the canine quiet and warm. Seek veterinary care immediately.

- **Snake Bites** – Snake venom typically immobilizes the victim and pre-digests the body tissues. In many cases, the victim's blood pressure will drop. In canines, the majority of bites occur on the head. The signs and symptoms include marked edema, swelling, redness, and immediate pain, subsiding after a couple of hours. Several hours after the bite, low blood pressure often occurs and in some cases respiratory distress. Bites occurring on the torso or neck should be considered more serious. Subdue and immobilize the canine, place gentle compression on the area, and transport immediately to a veterinarian.

- **Sprain** – Typically occurs when ligaments suddenly stretch or tear slightly. Joint injury can occur when fibers of supporting ligament are torn or ruptured. The symptoms include joint swelling and pain. Will normally heal within four weeks with rest.

- **Strain** – An overstretched or overexertion of some part of the muscle-tendon unit. This usually presents as a vague but painful lameness. Often there are no visible radiographic changes seen. Rest and anti-inflammatories are required for as long as 6-8 weeks.

- **Porcupine Quills** – If the quills are not removed promptly and completely, the canine could experience an infection or even death. When removing the quill be sure that the entire quill is removed. If the base of the quill breaks off, it could cause an abscess or migrate to a major organ, killing the canine. Be sure to include gums, tongue, ears and underbelly as you thoroughly and methodically check your canine for additional quills. Signs of this problem are the visible quills protruding from the skin, with inflammation and swelling. Because of the barbs found on the quills, removal should be conducted similarly to that of a fishhook, involving redirection and exposure of the barb for trimming. This may require sedation. Aspirin may be given for the inflammation, and an antibiotic may be needed for infection.

V. Candidate Study Guide – Lesson One (See Attachment I for Answers)

Take a few moments to complete the questions to identify where additional study may be necessary.

1. When a canine experiences heat stroke, the handler should immerse the canine in cool water.
   a. True
   b. False

2. Capillary Refill Time in healthy canines is less than 2 seconds.
   a. True
   b. False

3. The signs for canine bloat include:
   a. Distended abdomen
   b. Dry heaves
   c. Restlessness
   d. All of the above

4. What are the ABC's when assessing a canine to identify a life-threatening injury?
   a. Airway, blood, capillary refill
   b. Airway, breathing, circulation
   c. Airway, blood, circulation

5. To treat a _____, immobilize the area and transport the canine to a veterinarian.

6. _____ is the best body location to use to take a canine's pulse.

7. What is a normal temperature for a canine?
   a. 98.6F
   b. 99.7F
   c. 101-102.5F
   d. 103-105F

8. Snakebites that occur on a canine's torso or neck should be considered more serious than bites to other body parts.
   a. True
   b. False

9. Proper nutrition both at home and in the field are vital to the health and well being of the canine providing the nutrients and vitamins essential for stamina and endurance.
   a. True
   b. False

10. Canine hypothermia:
    a. Seldom occurs
    b. Must be treated as aggressively as human hypothermia
    c. Manifests with symptoms similar to human symptoms
    d. Requires minimal treatment
    e. a, d, c
    f. b, c

11. A _____ is an injury where fibers of supporting ligaments are torn or ruptured.

12. A _____ is an injury to the muscle-tendon unit.

13. Lethargy, labored breathing, pale gums and elevated heart rates are signs of
    _____.

14. It is safe to give a canine buffered aspirin.
    a. True
    b. False

15. Which of the following is NOT safe for a canine? (circle all that apply)
    a. Benadryl
    b. Motrin/Advil
    c. Pepto Bismol
    d. Tylenol

16. Bicipital tenosynovitis results from:
    a. Direct trauma
    b. Indirect trauma
    c. Overuse
    d. All of the above

Lesson Two

This lesson will help the candidate better understand the importance of obedience and agility in the field. It is not intended to endorse one type of training method over another. It will provide information on safety issues the candidate should consider during training. Additionally, the candidate will learn how obedience and agility transfer from training directly into the field.

I. Canine Obedience & Agility

You and your canine partner have just completed working a scene. As a reward, you take him to a grassy field to toss a ball. As the canine goes to retrieve the ball for the third time, his body language changes and he stops several feet from where it landed. Having observed the change in body language, you call the canine back to you. Once the canine is back at your side, you place the canine on a sit stay and walk over to the area where the ball landed. Upon reaching the area, you see that the ball is lying next to a rattlesnake. Your ability to read your canine's body language and your canine's response to your obedience commands prevented a possible snakebite.

Obedience is an important element of search and rescue work. No matter what discipline(s) a handler decides to pursue, a certain level of obedience training enhances the team's capabilities in the field. Even if a canine is to be worked on lead, obedience is necessary. Often handlers only see the necessity of obedience work for those canines working off lead, but obedience on lead is just as important both for safety reasons and to maintain a professional image. A canine that exits the vehicle and proceeds to the scene under control, then works enthusiastically and effectively upon command will more likely impress agencies. The public is more likely to receive or tolerate a well-mannered, under-control search canine. Finally, having on and off lead control of a search canine better ensures the safety of the canine, the handler, and the public.

Control and directability are two important benefits gained from obedience. Without the ability to direct a search canine, a search area might not be covered effectively. Consider a well-trained canine working a rubble pile after a major disaster. While on the rubble, the canine works in a controlled directional manner. The handler must work with the canine to cover the area without taking the canine's focus away from its work. The canine must be able to work independently to maneuver and problem-solve in the rubble to successfully discover scent.

Disaster work is not the only area where control and directability come into play. Whether working a homicide investigation in a small, specific area, working a "missing person" in a high traffic neighborhood, or searching for a lost hunter on several thousand acres, an off-lead canine should be under control with direction as necessary to cover the area effectively.

Obedience training also comes into play when a canine is asked to demonstrate for law enforcement agencies or the general public. During these demonstrations, the canine must display its socialization skills as well as its search and rescue capabilities. In addition, the canine should be friendly and non-aggressive around crowds, loud noises, and while being petted by numerous young people. It is during these situations that the canine's behavior will represent all other search and rescue canines in the eyes of the general public.

During demonstrations the handler is provided with opportunities to expose his canine to different types of distractions. The more the canine is exposed to distractions during training, the better prepared the canine will be to deal with the distractions it will face during an actual search. Sirens, cameras, people hustling back and forth, or simply being followed by numerous people as the canine works in the field could cause a canine to lose the focus it needs to do its job. By exposing the canine to these distractions during demonstrations and training, it will be better able to focus and work through distractions in the field. A canine that trains in a sterile setting may not be prepared for the distractions that occur during a search.

Agility training also plays an important role in search and rescue work. Unlike the American Kennel Club's (AKC) fast-paced competitive agility requiring rapid movement over obstacles, the search and rescue canine is taught to move slowly and deliberately over obstacles. The times when a SAR canine's agility will be most critical are during disaster or burned building searches. In order to remain safe, a canine must maneuver slowly and carefully through obstacles during its search. The canine should take its time to cover the area, and the handler should be able to guide the canine with directional signals to avoid unsafe areas.

Many different surfaces and obstacles should be incorporated into training. The canine should experience slick surfaces, un-sure footing, climbing different types of stairs and ladders, crawling through an object, and going over an object, just to name a few. A search and rescue canine ability course should include obstacles with specific field applications. Care should be given as to what obstacles provide practical and usable training. For example, a canine taught to jump through a window could inadvertently jump through a window while searching a building and plunge to its death. A purposeful design of a SAR agility course is a must.

In summary, the working search and rescue canine should possess excellent health, be obedient, agile, friendly, non-aggressive, focused, able to work through distractions and in a variety of terrain and weather conditions. Not all canines will be able to meet all of these criteria, but they most effectively define a true search and rescue canine.

II. Candidate Study Guide – Lesson Two (See Attachment I for Answers)

Take a few moments to complete the questions to identify where additional study may be necessary.

1. Rapid and ostentatious movements are considered important in training a canine for SAR related agility.
    a. True
    b. False

2. The type of agility apparatus you use in training should relate to what the canine will see on an actual search.
    a. True
    b. False

3. It is always good to teach a canine to indiscriminately jump over or through "open windows."
    a. True
    b. False

4. Agility practice can be a fun way to work on canine control as well as keeping your canine physically "tuned-up."
    a. True
    b. False

5. A well-socialized canine should:
    a. Accept all strangers
    b. Be willing to play with other canines
    c. Be friendly and non-aggressive
    d. Both a and b

6. Obedience training is only for those search and rescue canines that work off lead.
    a. True
    b. False

Lesson Three

This lesson will help the candidate better understand training logs, reading and building the canine's alert, private property issues and crime scene preservation. It is suggested that a candidate study how the "Good Samaritan" law applies, including specific stipulations that may prevent a handler and the canine from being protected by this law.

I. Handler Training Issues

Records

It is the responsibility of the handler to maintain the canine's training records. These records could be admissible in court should the handler ever be called upon to testify regarding the canine's work at a scene. The more searches a handler is involved in the greater the potential that he or she may end up in court. It is best to document training exercises as if planning to be called to take the witness stand.

An attorney examining training records should not only see what problems the canine had with exercises, but also what solutions the handler will adopt to help the canine work through any problems. Therefore, the training record should contain not only what the canine did right but also where the canine had problems and how those problems will be addressed in future training. Training records that only show what the canine did right could be used against the handler in court. Even though the prosecuting attorney can address the fact that there is no such thing as the perfect search and rescue canine, such records could nonetheless bring the handler and dog's credibility into question.

Canine Alerts

The handler should also be able to read the canine's body language and recognize the canine's alert. In court, the handler could be asked to explain what type of alert the canine gives or to demonstrate the canine's alert in the courtroom.

SAR canines can be trained to give many different kinds of alerts, so a handler should be knowledgeable regarding the different types. A scratch, bark, bringsel or re-find are all examples of trained alerts. A different alert can also be used for each type of discipline. There are times when one type of alert is more advantageous than another. When a canine locates a weapon, clothing or other items dropped by a lost person, it is preferred that the canine either bark or down at the item. In a wilderness setting where the canine is worked off lead, the canine might be taught to do a re-find, or return to the handler upon finding the subject, then re-find the subject with handler close behind. Regardless of the alert chosen, the handler must be able to intelligently explain the type of alert his canine gives and have it documented throughout the training records.

It is also extremely important that the handler know if the canine has given a "false alert," or is presenting the alert behavior with no valid find. In the event the canine does give a false alert, the handler should document this in the training record and work toward correcting this problem. The handler should make sure he or she is not inadvertently cueing the false alert through hand or body movements or by talking the canine into an alert. There are times on a scene when a handler can be predisposed to believe the subject will be found in a specific area. A proven canine may previously have indicated there, or agency personnel may strongly believe the subject will be located there. This is when a false alert most commonly occurs--when a handler wants his canine to be right by alerting where he "believes" the subject will be located. Instead, the handler should allow the canine to work the area with sufficient time and only call an alert if the canine truly indicates one. Should a properly trained canine not indicate a find after thoroughly working an area, the handler should be confident enough to state the area cleared.

The canine handler should document everything –the good, the bad, and the ugly—and the paperwork will be looked upon as a valid training record in court. Clear, concise records will aid in avoiding confusion, misinterpretation, and present a clear representation of the dog and handler's abilities.

II. Search Scene Considerations

The agencies that call upon the volunteer search and rescue handler expect a certain level of professionalism and knowledge. There are important protocols of which a handler must be aware when working with requesting agencies at a scene, including those pertaining to handler liability, radio communications, and crime scene preservation. A handler should obtain training in these and other areas before responding to a scene for the first time.

Handler Liability

When on scene, a handler is not automatically covered against the threat of lawsuit by a requesting agency. Many responders feel that their actions are protected from litigation by Good Samaritan Laws. A quick search of the Internet can provide individual state's versions of the law. One site provides a clear explanation: "Good Samaritan laws are laws aimed at protecting from blame those who choose to aid others who are injured or ill in the United States" (retrieved 05/09/05).

It is important to understand that the "Good Samaritan" law does not prevent lawsuits but is intended to give legal protection for volunteer emergency services. Handlers should know the limitations of the "Good Samaritan" law as it pertains to their actions in their state. In some instances, the "Good Samaritan" law might not cover a handler who claims expertise. Search and rescue personnel should be very careful in any situation in which they may be providing services for which they have not been trained or certified. It is the responsibility of the handler to know the laws that govern this issue for each state in which he or she provides volunteer services.

A handler may be able to limit liability by completing training which meets widely-recognized standards, such as NASAR's Canine SARTECH^{TM} Certification, and by documenting all activities and maintaining current liability insurance. Verifiable training and testing criteria and documentation that the handler and canine successfully completed the designated requirements can help reduce the handler's liability.

19

Search Scene Procedures

The handler is responsible for understanding the requesting agency's expectations. In addition to specific agency procedures that should be followed in the field, there are some general procedures that should always be observed, including:

- There are two acceptable ways a handler could enter private property during a search when working in the field: (1) when there is reasonable certainty that life may be in danger; or (2) with the consent of the property owner or their agent. A handler could be considered to be trespassing on private property if one of these criteria is not met.

- If the handler locates a possible clue while working a scene, he or she should transmit the clue location and description to Command via radio. It is the decision of Command as to whether the item should be bagged and transported or left in place, well flagged and marked on the map. If the decision is to flag the clue, it is suggested three (3) pieces of flagging tape marked with the handler's name, the date and time, and task assignment number if applicable be utilized to clearly mark the area.

- The handler must understand the *chain of evidence*—the documented series of individuals and agencies that come in contact with a piece of evidence. In order for a piece of evidence to be considered viable the date, time, individual's name, rank and agency affiliation must be documented on the evidence log sheet each time the evidence changes hands. The chain begins with the individual who originally found the evidence and ends when it is finally logged in at the agency's evidence room. Thus finding a clue, then abandoning it for any length of time, may be grounds for or result in refusal of the evidence in court. The handler locating a piece of evidence in the field should turn the item over to the controlling agency's law enforcement officer. The handler's notes should reflect a description of the clue, the location, the time located, and the name of the officer to whom the evidence was given. It is then the responsibility of the recipient to maintain the proper documentation as the evidence makes its way to its final destination.

If the handler/dog team locates a deceased subject or there is the slightest indication that there may be foul play involved, the team should back out of the area the way they entered, in an effort not to alter the scene. The handler should also control the area by keeping others out and turn the scene over to the proper authorities as soon as possible. Upon transferring the scene, the handler should note the name of the law enforcement officer and the time the scene was turned over. The handler is also responsible for specifying where (s)he walked, what (s)he touched and whether (s)he left anything within the crime scene.

III. Candidate Study Guide – Lesson Three (See Attachment I for Answers)

Take a few moments to complete the questions to identify where additional study may be necessary.

1. The maintenance of training records is the responsibility of the team secretary.
    a. True
    b. False

2. It's all right to leave a clue unattended if only for a short time.
    a. True
    b. False

3. Proper procedure when finding a clue does not include:
    a. Flagging the area with 3 pieces of flagging tap marked with your name, the date and time, and task assignment number if applicable
    b. Transmitting the clue location and description to base via radio
    c. Noting the wind direction
    d. Marking the clue on a map

4. Your training records should only show what your canine does proficiently.
    a. True
    b. False

5. The "Good Samaritan" law prevents lawsuits for all volunteers.
    a. True
    b. False

6. Your exposure to liability can be reduced by
    a. Training to a recognized standard
    b. Documenting all activities
    c. Maintaining current liability insurance
    d. All of the above

7. A canine handler should be well-trained and proficient in:
    a. Reading his/her canine and recognizing its alert
    b. Handling the press so that everyone will know they were on the scene
    c. Using proper search terms
    d. Both a and c

8. Entry onto private property may be justified during a search when:
    a. Obtaining the permission of the property owner or their agent
    b. SAR personnel are in uniform and have responded as a state resource
    c. There is a reasonable certainty that life may be in danger
    d. Both a and c

Lesson Four

The candidate should be able to explain scent theory and how environmental factors affect scent. The candidate should also be able to explain the differences between air scenting, tracking/trailing, scent discrimination and how best to utilize each. Finally, the candidate should be able to explain how scent articles are gathered and used.

I. Scent Theory

Scent Production

The generally accepted theory of scent transport developed by Bill Syrotuck (1972) describes human "scent particles" as "rafts" of shed skin cells, respiratory, and digestive tract cells. The shape and size of a raft allows it to float on air currents. On average, each carries four microbial passengers. The character Pigpen in the popular comic strip by Charles Schulz has often illustrated the scent picture. Just as Pigpen walks around with a cloud of dust surrounding him, we humans have a cloud of skin rafts surrounding us. It is believed that the rafts, with their passenger bacteria, produce unique signature odors enabling canines to discriminate between one human being and another. This is called *discriminatory-humanoid evidence*. The composition of this cloud of skin rafts varies with heredity, race, culture and personal hygiene.

Sweat glands differ between races. African-Americans have a greater number of total sweat glands and larger-sized apocrine glands (large sweat glands associated with hair follicles). Caucasians have fewer total sweat glands and apocrine secretions vary from one individual to another between clear and turbid. Asians have the least number of sweat glands.

Studies have shown that humans have a current of air next to the skin surface estimated to be traveling at a rate of 125 feet per minute or 1.42 miles per hour. The current begins at the feet and travels up the body until it comes off the top of the head. Some of the rafts fall where a person walks while the rest are carried some distance from the source on air currents. The distance the rafts travel depends upon wind velocity, vegetation and terrain features.

Syrotuck states that heredity provides individual differences on the cellular level. With the possible exception of identical twins, each human has a unique genetic scent component. Besides the scent components of a particular individual—cells, skin secretions, and bacteria—there are environmental factors—which affect the total *scent picture*. Temperature and humidity affect the bacteria decomposing the raft and thus the scent (vapor cloud) it produces. Atmospheric factors produce wind currents both close to and at some distance above the ground. Terrain features can affect the movement of wind and air currents. All of these can affect scent distribution. Thus, condition of the subject, environment, and atmosphere must be considered together for the handler to understand the scent picture and how it is changing.

Olfactory Senses

The olfactory system is comprised of the nasal chambers and sinuses. It gathers scent while the olfactory nerves carry signals to the olfactory lobe that is located in the brain. It is the olfactory lobe that actually recognizes the odors. Almost an eighth of the canine brain, and over 50% of the internal canine nose is dedicated to olfaction.

The canine has the ability to distinguish between multiple scents whereas humans are unable to do so. For example, when a person enters a bakery, he or she is inundated with sweet smells. However, after a few moments the person becomes accustomed to the odors and will no longer smell it. The canine however, not only can distinguish between all the different bakery goods, but also can smell each ingredient being used in the bakery and will not become accustomed to the smell. This is why the canine can smell a scent article belonging to one individual and follow that specific scent through all other scents in the search area. It is this innate sense that allows the canine to excel in search and rescue work.

Environmental Factors Affecting Scent
Several environmental factors can affect the canine's capability to detect scent: wind, temperature, time of day, rain/snow, humidity, ground-level temperature, and the subject's body temperature. The handler should keep these factors in mind whether working a problem during training or officially deployed on a search.

Principles and strategies to consider when working should include the following:

(1) **Temperature affects scent.** During hot weather, working at first light will help the canine as the cooler air and the night's dew will help enhance scent. Temperature can either promote or destroy the rafts. During hot weather, the moisture within the raft cells quickly dries up causing the bacteria on the raft to become dormant. A minute vapor cloud, resulting from the bacteria using the raft as a nutrient, surrounds bacteria-laden rafts. Once that vapor cloud is destroyed by heat, the bacteria no longer have the nutrients needed to thrive. Therefore, in hot, dry weather, ground scenting is difficult. An infusion of humidity will re-hydrate the rafts allowing the bacteria to begin multiplying rapidly, producing a stronger scent intensity.

(2) **Humidity and precipitation affect scent**. Humidity affects scent by generally increasing its availability--reviving scent that has "dried out" by restoring bacterial activity. The time of day the trail is laid is important. As humidity and temperature change during the day, the rafts—and scent—on a trail are affected. If the trail is laid in the early afternoon on a hot day, the rafts will quickly begin drying up. As dew forms in the evening hours, the moisture will reactivate the bacterial activity, thus re-hydrating the rafts providing them with their food supply. The bacteria will multiply quickly and will provide more scent than when the trail was originally laid. The level of scent would be at its highest during the late evening when the dew and lower temperatures promote higher scent intensity. Heavy rain can wash away the scent.

(3) **Wind transports scent**, moving rafts along the path of least resistance. If a subject is hidden in a wooded area just off a roadway and the prevailing wind is blowing from the woods toward the roadway, the roadway will tend to channel air and scent along its path.

(4) **Time of day can affect scent** through changing humidity levels, temperature, and air movement. Scent will rise in the morning and fall in the afternoon. Therefore, if a handler is working a hilltop or mountainous area, he will want to work the hilltop in the morning and the valley in the evening. This will provide the canine with the best-case scenario for picking up scent. This effect can be seen on area ponds and waterways. In the early morning hours note the fog that may be coming off of the top of the water. As the morning progresses, it will stop rising and begin moving with the wind before dropping and finally dissipating altogether. On a trail laid during the evening hours, the bacterial process is slowed down by the lower (below-optimum) temperature at night. The following morning the raft is regenerated from the dew, and as the temperature rises, the bacterial activity also increases, generating greater scent intensity.

By better understanding how weather affects transportation of scent, handlers can better plan search strategy. The following will provide a general explanation of how these issues affect canines in the field.

Stability of the atmosphere is determined by the cooling rate of air as it rises into the atmosphere, humidity levels, and the presence of inversions (when a layer of warm air moves over the top of a layer of cold air). Simply stated, if the rising surface air temperature matches the atmospheric temperature quickly, the air is stable. If the rising air remains warmer and lighter than the surrounding air and thus continues to rise, the air is unstable.

Inversions create an extremely stable air situation that can block air movement, and therefore, scent transport. Inversions generally occur at night, and can be associated with terrain, often occurring in valley bottoms. A good indicator of an inversion is when the air temperature gets warmer rather than colder when moving uphill. Because there is little air movement, scent will pool at the bottom of the inversion making it difficult to determine where the scent is originating. The inversion will lift when the sun comes up or the air warms, but the timing is unpredictable. When the inversion breaks up, the winds will be erratic as the cool and warm air layers begin mixing.

Humidity will affect air stability because moist air loses heat less rapidly than dry air. As a result, the rising parcel of humid air tends to remain warmer than the surrounding atmospheric air for a longer interval of elevation gain.

When the air is stable, stratus-type clouds in layers without vertical motion may be visible. It may be foggy or hazy if the wind speed is slow, and the winds will be steady. Depending on wind speed, the wind will follow contours of obstacles it encounters. When the air is unstable, clouds will grow vertically and cumulus-type clouds may be visible. Dust devils indicate surface air instability. Instability is also indicated by the presence of lines of clouds.

24

Sandy Bryson (1991) describes five general scent-plume patterns that are dependent on what the wind is doing. The scent-plumes may be subtle and may occur at transition times between primary wind patterns.

- **Looping** occurs when there is a high degree of convective turbulence caused by instability both at the surface and aloft. The surface air rises rapidly, cools quickly, and falls back to the surface repeating this pattern.

- Scent transport at sunrise is characterized as **Fumigating**. Fumigating occurs when stable air aloft and unstable air at the surface combine as the surface air quickly warms, and the scent plume diffuses down through the warmer air. It is this condition that offers the best scent at daybreak.

- **Lofting** is the opposite of fumigating. It occurs when there is stable surface air and unstable air. This occurs after sunset as the ground is cooling and the air aloft is still warm. Because the unstable air aloft is pulling the surface air upwards, on calm evenings it may be best to work ridges if there is no prevailing down slope wind.

- **Coning** occurs on cloud-covered days or nights. The air moves about in a cone-like fashion. Coning is an ideal scent condition where scent stays low to the ground forming a cone shape with the subject located at the point of the cone and spreading out from the subject based upon the wind. It should be noted that the term "Coning" is also used to describe the zigzag pattern a dog follows to the victim once it has detected scent.

- **Fanning** occurs in stable air as a result of an inversion layer on calm clear nights just before sunrise. The scent cone compresses vertically, but is spread horizontally. Scent may be out of the dog's range if the dog is at a lower or higher elevation than where the scent is fanning out.

- **Chimney Effect** occurs during the daytime when the cooler air in a wooded area is drawn vertically by warming air through an opening in a timber. If a handler and canine are walking down a road at mid-day with the wind coming out of the woods where a subject is located inside the wood line, the canine may fail to locate the subject because of the chimney effect. The handler should recognize the conditions that contribute to this phenomenon in order to effectively help the canine work through the problem.

Note: See Attachment II for Scent Pattern Illustrations.

Wind speeds can affect scent dispersal. The Beaufort scale can assist a handler in determining wind velocity in the field. The scale provides the handler with a tabular description of how environmental factors react to different wind speeds as indicated in the table that follows.

Table 1 – Beaufort Scale

Force	Description	Result	Wind Speed (mph)	(knots)
0	Calm	Smoke rises vertically	0 – 1	<1
1	Light Air	Wind direction indicated by smoke but not wind vanes	1 – 5	1 - 3
2	Light breeze	Wind noticeable, leaves move, wind vane moves.	6 – 11	4 - 6
3	Gentle breeze	Leaves and small twigs in constant motion.	12 – 19	7 - 10
4	Moderate breeze	Wind raises dust and loose paper. Small branches are moved.	20 – 29	11 - 16
5	Fresh breeze	Small trees in leaf start to sway. Crested wavelets form on inland waters.	30 – 39	17 - 21
6	Strong breeze	Large branches in motion, wind whistles. Umbrellas used with difficulty.	40 – 50	22 - 27
7	Near gale	Trees in motion, awkward to walk against wind.	51 – 61	28 - 33
8	Gale	Twigs break, hard to walk.	62 – 74	34 - 40
9	Strong gale	Some structural damage may occur, slates removed etc.	75 – 87	41 - 47
10	Storm	Trees uprooted, considerable structural damage.	88 – 101	48 - 55
11	Violent storm	Widespread damage.	102 – 117	56 - 63
12	Hurricane	Widespread damage.	118+	> 63

Air Scenting, Tracking, and Trailing

The main components in the creation of a scent trail are airborne rafts shed by the subject, physical disturbance of earth, and crushed vegetation (where present) from the subject's footsteps. These occur in some combination as a person walks through an area, and are the factors the search canine uses to locate the subject. The basic difference between air scenting, tracking, and trailing is the path the dog takes to reach the subject. Air scent, borne on the wind, might not be physically located close to the person's track—consequently an air scenting canine may follow the scent trail some distance from the track, and, given the opportunity, will follow the scent cone directly to the source without necessarily traversing any part of the track. An air-scenting canine mainly utilizes airborne rafts to work out the scent picture, and his head will be high, always checking the wind.

A tracking canine works from human scent, crushed vegetation, and physical disturbance of the earth occurring right at the individual's footprint. His nose will be down, and his path will follow exactly where the footprints occur without varying more than one or two feet.

A trailing canine will follow the scent from rafts that have fallen to the ground around, but not necessarily on the track. Depending on the wind strength, he will normally follow at some distance lateral to the track, where the rafts/scent have drifted. The tracking/trailing canine should follow a relatively fresh trail in the direction of the subject's travel, moving from less intense scent to more intense scent.

Scent Discrimination

Whether air scenting, trailing or tracking, a canine can be considered as human *detecting* if it is trained to look for <u>any</u> human, while the *discriminating* canine is taught to make use of a scent article and will only locate the person whose scent is on the article.

When a person's foot makes an impression in the earth, crushed vegetation releases fluids, vapor enshrouded rafts come to rest on the ground, and bacterial decomposition of the crushed plant cells begins. It is the dead plant vapors that are considered *non-discriminatory evidence*.

Considerations for Training Trailing, Tracking, and Air Scent

When setting up trailing training exercises, the handler should be sure to start the canine moving in a different direction than the subject's initial trail in order to teach the canine that how to locate the trail. On *heat-aged trails*, it is best to lay the trail in the morning and work the canine in the late afternoon. This allows the trail to bake in the midday sun and be run in the late afternoon before cooling ages the track. A trail laid in the evening and run in the morning may age in time, but is regenerating scent through the cooler parts of the day.

When setting up air scent problems, the problem should be set up to encourage the canine to air scent rather than track (e.g., starting the canine from a different point from where the subject started). To increase the likelihood of picking up scent in the field, the handler should train the canine to range back and forth in the field, one way to teach this is for the handler to zigzag across the field until the canine learns the pattern.

When training any search canine to utilize scent articles, the articles should be chosen carefully. During training, the scent articles initially used should be made of cloth, as they tend to hold a higher level of scent than many other materials. As training progresses, the handler should include scent articles made of metal, wood, plastic, etc. Some materials will hold less scent than others--however, the canine should be trained to work using all types, as one never knows what will be available at an actual search scene.

Scent Articles

A canine can be trained to use a scent article to locate a specific individual. It is important that the handler know how the scent article was obtained, who may have handled it, etc.

Proper technique for handling a scent article is necessary:

- The scent article should be picked out with the family present to make sure the missing individual last wore the article selected.
- Look for items with which other family members have not come in contact.
- When picking up the article, make sure gloves are worn and a bag is available in which to place the article.
- All attempts should be made to keep the scent article as pure as possible.

- It is always best if handlers are allowed to pick and bag the scent articles they use in order to help protect the integrity of the clue.

The quality of the scent article is important:
- Determine whether or not the scent article actually belongs to the subject and if they were the only one to wear or touch the item.
- Be sure that the subject's scent article did not come out of the family clothes hamper.
- Determine how the scent article was handled. Was it picked up by a family member in their hands and placed in a bag, was it picked up by a volunteer or deputy who placed the article under their arm to carry it out of the home, or was the article picked out by someone other than a family member after going into the subject's room and deciding what to use?
- Some of the best scent articles are made of natural fibers, are worn close to the skin and have been packaged without being touched. By keeping this in mind when looking for the perfect scent article, the handler will be providing the canine with the best-case scenario for picking up the correct scent.

An item belonging to the subject and properly bagged could mean the difference between success and failure.

II. Candidate Study Guide – Lesson Four (See Attachment I for Answers)

Take a few moments to complete the questions to identify where additional study may be necessary.

1. _____ and _____ are two pieces of evidence present when a person walks through a vegetated area.

2. Temperature can either promote or destroy rafts.
   a. True
   b. False

3. Wind, temperature and humidity are considered:
   a. Environmental factors
   b. Human make-up factors
   c. None of the above

4. Generally, increased humidity revives and increases the availability of scent.
   a. True
   b. False

5. Terrain and man-made obstacles affect how scent is carried/distributed by the wind.
   a. True
   b. False

6. During the middle of a hot sunny day, scent will tend to:
   a. Rise straight up
   b. Collect in low places
   c. Stick to leaves and grass
   d. All of the above

7. Scent transport at sunrise is characterized as fanning.
   a. True
   b. False

8. The Beaufort Scale measures
   a. Distance on a topo map
   b. Relative humidity
   c. Air temperature
   d. Wind velocity

9. A *human discriminating* canine is oriented to:
   a. A specific human being without any clues
   b. A specific piece of evidence
   c. A specific human being via some scent article, such as an article of clothing

10. A *human detecting* canine is cued to:
    a. A specific human being
    b. Specific articles
    c. "Any" human being

11. When using a scent article, the handler should know the following:
    a. Type of scent article
    b. How article was packaged
    c. Who obtained the scent article
    d. How it was determined that the article belongs to the subject
    e. All of the above

12. Fanning is best described as:
    a. A treatment for canine heat stroke
    b. A ground team search pattern for covering a triangular search area in high winds
    c. Occurring in high wind conditions on cloudy days just before sunset
    d. Occurring in stable air as a result of an inversion layer on calm clear nights just before sunrise

13. An air scent canine is:
    a. A search canine that will locate the scent of a specific individual
    b. A canine that will detect airborne human scent
    c. A search canine that will follow almost exactly the ground scent track of a person
    d. Both a and b

14. One way to teach a canine to loop around you or to range back and forth in front of you is to:
    e. Zigzag back and forth yourself until the canine gets the idea
    f. Walk the canine, on leash, in circles or in a zigzag pattern
    g. Teach a zigzag command

15. To encourage a canine to airscent rather than track, search problems should be arranged so that the canine starts in a different place from the track of the victim.
    h. True
    i. False

16. A _____ canine works with a scent article and may range several feet from the actual track.

17. A _____ canine does not vary more than two feet from the victim's footsteps and works with head down.

Lesson Five

The candidate should know the protocols for safely approaching and loading onto a helicopter, flight protocol, and departure safety, and be able to discuss equipment for both the handler and his canine partner.

I. Helicopter Safety

We will take a few moments to discuss some of the key safety and training issues a handler should understand. Before a handler ever embarks on a helicopter with his/her canine, (s)he should first have a clear understanding of the rules. Prior to flight time, a handler and canine should go through training with the pilot and ground crew regarding signals and other safety measures. It is the pilot of the helicopter that is in control of the entry and departure of the crew and passengers and has total say in how crew and passengers load and unload from the helicopter. The ground crew will indicate the position in which each handler and canine will stand while waiting for the pilot's signal to load. The proper distance to maintain when not loading is at least 100 feet from the helicopter.

Side-loading helicopters (e.g., Dolphins)
The loading position is usually located at the 3:00 position from the front of the helicopter (The front of the helicopter is the 12:00 position while the rear of the helicopter is the 6:00 position). It is a position where the pilot is able to see the handler, and the handler can approach from the front of the helicopter instead of the rear. At no time should a crewmember or passenger ever enter or depart from the rear. This is one safety rule that is strongly enforced by both the ground crew and pilot.

Back-loading helicopters (e.g., Chinooks)
Loading position is at 6:00, through the rear of the aircraft.

Procedures for Helicopter Training Exercises
Upon a signal from the pilot, the crew will then signal the handler when to load.

The pilot will explain where each handler should sit and how to buckle up. It is up to the handler to make sure that his canine is totally under control and placed in a position that will not impair the function of the crew or interfere with other handlers and canines. Once everything is explained and questions are answered, then each handler and canine should practice loading on and off the helicopter without the engines and rotors engaged. At this time the handler should be observing the canine's behavior in the location and position for flight (in sit or down position).

In the next phase of the helicopter training the engines and rotors should be engaged, with the handlers and canines positioned approximately 100 feet from the helicopter. It is helpful for the handler to kneel next to the canine when the engines and rotors are initiated. The handler should observe the canine's behavior. If the canine attempts to pull away, the handler should gently encourage the canine to settle down and accept the noise and wind from the helicopters engines and rotors. If the canine will not settle down, the handler should remove the canine from the area. This particular canine is just not mentally ready for this type of training. The handler might try again weeks or months later, but should never force the canine to accept the helicopter. If forced, the canine will never be comfortable, and this could possibly cause a problem during a future flight.

If all goes well, the handler and canine are ready for the final step, the actual loading, flight, and unloading. As the handler steps forward to the predetermined position, (s)he should have a short grip on his canine's lead and be prepared for the canine's reaction to the down or rotorwash (moving air generated from spinning rotors) that occurs halfway between the tips of the rotors and the entrance to the helicopter. Normally, if the handler moves confidently forward to the helicopter, the canine may pause briefly under the rotorwash and then continue forward. Should the canine react strongly to the rotorwash, the handler should attempt to move the canine quickly through it.

Once inside the compartment, the handler should continue monitoring his canine for stress and anxiety. If either of these conditions occurs, the handler should reassure and calm the canine. If the situation shows signs of worsening, the handler should make the pilot aware and request that they return to base. Under no circumstances should the handler wait too long to make this call in hopes of getting the canine to eventually relax. The pilot and crew will have more respect for a handler who makes this call early on than one who allows his canine to become stressed enough to become aggressive.

Upon landing, the pilot will give passengers a signal when it is safe to depart the helicopter. Each handler on the flight should depart in a controlled and safe manner. Keeping a good grip on the canine's lead, the handler should exit the compartment, moving straight out from the doorway making sure to move in the correct direction from the helicopter. Once again the handler should be prepared for the rotorwash.

Helicopter training offers a wonderful opportunity for both the handler and canine, but it is also another situation in which the search and rescue canine will be under the magnifying glass. It is extremely important that a search and rescue canine's temperament and comfort zone in tight, noisy environments will not be an issue. A search and rescue canine that attacks a crew member or other passenger is totally unacceptable and could result in *all* search and rescue canines being permanently refused for future training.

II. Canine Equipment

Just as a handler would not consider entering snowy woods dressed in summer clothing, neither should the canine enter the field without proper equipment. In wilderness or urban settings, the canine may wear a properly fitted tracking harness or shabrack (search vest). In a disaster setting it is safer for the canine not to wear any equipment at all, as it may become snagged on debris.

Items a handler carries in the 24-hour ready pack should include extra food and water if the team be going into an area where there is the possibility of staying out all night. In all situations, the handler should carry extra water to cool a heated canine -- especially true when working during very hot weather. Along with food and water, the handler's pack should contain necessary first aid, change of clothing and items that can be used for shelter and basic survival needs. A periodic check of pack contents should be done in order to replace those items used during a previous search. A list of items that the handler should carry into the field can be downloaded from the NASAR website at www.nasar.org. The candidate will have to show the contents of this list to the evaluator during the classroom session as part of the certification requirements.

III. Candidate Study Guide – Lesson Five (See Attachment I for Answers)

Take a few moments to complete the questions to identify where additional study may be necessary.

1. Prior to exiting a helicopter, the handler should:
    a. Wait for a signal from the pilot
    b. Wait for the rotors to stop
    c. Wave to everyone on the ground awaiting the helicopter's arrival

2. In a wilderness or urban setting, the handler may opt to have the canine wear a properly fitted harness or shabrack (vest).
    a. True
    b. False

3. When will the handler and canine experience downwash from a helicopter?
    a. When the helicopter is sitting idle on the runway
    b. As the helicopter takes off
    c. As the helicopter lands
    d. As the handler and canine reach the midway point under the moving rotor blades

4. The ground crew and pilot are in charge of helicopter loading and departure.
    a. True
    b. False

5. The proper distance that one should maintain from the helicopter when not loading is:
    a. 100 feet
    b. 200 feet
    c. 300 feet
    d. 25 yards

6. The 24-hour ready pack should include the following:
    a. Clothing, food and first aid
    b. Snacks, games and reading materials
    c. Water, clothing and books

7. It is acceptable for a canine to growl at the crewmembers during a helicopter flight.
    a. True
    b. False

Lesson Six

The purpose of this lesson is to identify search strategies that a handler should consider during training and searches. How wind and other factors affect the scenario will also be discussed. It is important that handlers train in all different weather conditions, terrain features and times of day. In some cases, the handler may wish to attend training seminars outside the area in order to experience totally different types of terrain and weather conditions.

I. Search Strategy

Search strategies a handler can use to cover an assigned area include *hasty*, *grid*, and *contour* strategies. Refer to Lesson 4 for review of coning, lofting, fumigating, fanning, chimney effect and other conditions that affect distribution of scent.

Often a handler will begin a search by doing a hasty search. Searching trails, roads, pathways, the area of point last seen (PLS), and the area of highest probability of detection (POD) are all areas where a hasty search should be considered. The hasty search covers a great deal of high probability area rapidly. It is also a great way to allow high drive canines to work off some of their energy before being asked to settle down to a more methodical and detailed approach. When clearing a small grid without an appropriate map, the handler may opt to do a hasty search of the grid in an effort to provide information about the terrain features of the search area. This information will help determine how to cover the area in a more efficient manner.

A grid search entails both handler and canine moving in a sweeping pattern across an assigned area. Typically, an air scent canine best works when sweeping across the wind. The air scent handler will sweep or zigzag back and forth from one boundary to the next. Each sweep, or grid, is spaced out from the next a certain distance. This distance is calculated using the wind speed, weather conditions, terrain, and vegetative features.

Contour searching requires the search canine and handler to move along the side of a terrain feature at a particular elevation, indicated by contour lines on a topographical map. The handler must design the search strategy to best use the wind movement as outline in Lesson 4. Thus, a canine team may sweep across a terrain feature following contour lines, each successive sweep either higher or lower on the land feature.

Terrain features and time of day will largely determine how an area should be covered. In areas where the terrain is flat and featureless, a hasty and/or grid search is best—the terrain often allows good air movement, which allows the canine and handler to cover the area in a grid pattern. A hilly or mountainous area might be better searched utilizing a contour strategy. A few scenarios best illustrate appropriate search strategies:

A handler has been asked to cover 70 acres of flat, featureless terrain. It is 0730 hours and the temperature is 50 degrees F. The wind is out of the west at 5 mph. The handler should take into account the wind and temperature factors. With the low wind and temperature factors, it would be more advantageous to use a grid pattern working North to South. Scent will travel a short distance from the subject and will not be affected by any terrain features that could serve as a catch (such as a drainage feature or ridge).

In comparison, if asked to cover 40 acres with well-defined ridges and drainages at 0200 hours with temperatures in the 50's F and light variable winds, the handler would want to take into account that the drainages would serve as a catch feature for scent. With variable winds, a hasty search starting in the drainages would be the most beneficial search strategy. At that time of day, scent will be traveling down from the ridges gathering in the drainages. By working the drainages, the handler will be able to determine if the subject is above on the ridge.

In another scenario, a handler is presented with an area having well-defined ridges and drainages, it is 1000 hours, and the temperature is 60 degrees F with light and variable winds. In this scenario, the best search strategy would be to do a contour, starting on the ridges, as scent should be traveling upward. The handler should start on the high ground where the canine can pick up the scent as it rises.

Generally, in early morning as the air on the top of ridges or hilltops warms, it will rise, to be replaced by the cooler air from the drainages and valleys. (As is often the case, variations can occur on east slopes versus west slopes and in other cases.) Therefore in the morning, scent will travel upward to the tops of the ridges. In the afternoon, the opposite happens, the hot valley air rises and is replaced with cooler air from the ridges. Up in the morning, down in the evening. It is this effect that handlers should consider when setting up their search strategy in that type of terrain.

Lofting occurs after sunset when the surface experiences stable air while the unstable air is aloft. When this occurs, the canine should be worked at sunset on top of ridges to better pick up scent.

In fumigating conditions, which are the opposite of lofting, stable air aloft and unstable air at the surface combines, the surface air quickly warms, and the cooler scent plume diffuses down through the warmer air. It is advantageous to work the canine at sunrise, as the scent will gather along the bottom of the ridges and in drainage areas. Additionally, scent could gather along power lines, roadways, rivers, or fence lines, as each of these will help hold scent for the canine.

The only times a handler should discontinue coverage of his or her assigned area are when the subject is found, or if the area becomes too dangerous for the handler and canine to continue, or if re-assigned or re-called by Command.

II. Other Strategic Considerations

This section describes some common situations a handler could encounter during a search and how best to handle each situation.

There will be times when a canine will shows high interest and circles an area several times, but is unable to work out the problem. If on an actual search, the handler should consider working the canine out in ever expanding circles from area of interest. If the canine is still unable to work it out, the handler should mark his map with the location of the "interest" area, including the wind direction and time. The handler should complete the search. During debrief the Incident Commander (IC) should be made aware of the high interest areas.

A handler may hear over the radio that another handler's canine has strong alerts or has picked up scent. (S)he should not stop searching the assigned area until the subject is confirmed to be found. Nor should handlers in adjacent areas move to the area where the alerts occur or scent is being picked up. There is always a possibility of the subject crossing over from one area to another. Therefore, if a handler leaves the assigned area uncovered, the subject could potentially be missed or found later in the unfinished area.

If one handler/canine team is working on one ridge of a valley upwind from another team on the next ridge of the valley and the second team is experiencing strong alerts but is unsuccessful at working them out, the first handler should consider that the second canine maybe alerting on him or her. The first handler should inform the second handler of that possibility, as all are there to work together to assist in locating the missing subject.

37

III. Candidate Study Guide – Lesson Six (See Attachment I for Answers)

Take a few moments to complete the questions to identify where additional study may be necessary.

1. When training, the handler should:
    a. Work only when the weather is cool enough not to stress the canine
    b. Train only in early morning or early evening
    c. Train in a variety of terrains and weather conditions
    d. Train a minimum of three times per week
    e. Both b and d.

2. You are working below a 60-foot cliff in your sector. Your canine is alerting 20 yards from the cliff but as you get close to the cliff the canine looses the scent. You have determined the wind is coming from the direction of the cliff face. What is the most likely location of the subject?
    a. On top of cliff
    b. Between where your canine is alerting and the cliff
    c. You have passed them and they are behind you
    d. The canine is not alerting on the subject

3. Trails, roads, pathways, the area of point last seen, and the area of highest probability of detection are all areas where a hasty search should be considered.
    a. True
    b. False

4. Fumigating conditions should be worked early in the evening.
    a. True
    b. False

5. In areas that have flat and featureless terrain, it is best to:
    a. Use a contour search pattern
    b. Conduct a hasty search
    c. Use a grid pattern

6. Hasty, contour, and grid are considered what?
    a. Search strategies
    b. Map readings
    c. Topographical map markings

7. In the morning, scent travels _____.

8. In the evening, scent travels _____.

9. Lofting conditions should be worked at sunset.
   a. True
   b. False

10. If a handler's assigned grid is too dangerous to cover, the handler should:
    a. Slowly back out in order not to disturb anything
    b. Finish clearing the grid anyway, so people don't think the handler is not capable of clearing the grid
    c. Radio to the Incident Commander to make them aware of the danger
    d. Clear the area, but think "safety" while doing so

11. As a canine handler, you are the most important part of the search operations. Therefore you should be given special treatment at the scene.
    a. True
    b. False

12. Drainages, rivers and fence lines are all considered what?
    a. Natural grid borders
    b. Catching features
    c. Obstacles to cross

Lesson Seven

This lesson addresses the importance of working as part of a team on a search. Understanding how all teams interface and of the terminology commonly used at a scene will assist handlers in their efforts to be team players. Additionally, lost person behaviors and the importance of knowing as much as possible about the subject will be discussed.

I. Interfacing the Support Team and the Canine Team

There are times when canine handlers will need to work with backups/flankers/walkers who have never before worked a search. In this circumstance, it is the responsibility of the handler to quickly educate these individuals on their responsibilities in the field. A working relationship should be developed by taking a few moments to explain such things as not walking ahead of the canine, being on the lookout for clues and signs and assisting with navigational issues, including marking areas of interest on a map. There are times when support team members may be asked to assist in carrying extra water or in radio operations. Because the backups/flankers/walkers are part of the canine field team, the handler should make sure that they are never abandoned in the field.

It is the responsibility of the canine team to assist in locating the subject, locating clues, and clearing areas. There are times when a canine will not locate the subject because it was not assigned to the area where the subject was located. If the canine is able to effectively clear its area, it has done its job, whether or not it directly locates the subject. Not everyone on a scene will make the find, however it takes all parties working together to bring about a successful conclusion to a search.

II. Communications

Every handler should possess knowledge of basic radio terminology and etiquette. The minimum power level that enables effective communications should be used (it is not always necessary to have the highest-powered radio available). If having difficulty "closing the link," a handler should consider moving to higher terrain, changing the battery, using a higher power level, or requesting a relay. The handler should refrain from the temptation to turn up the volume control in an attempt to increase transmission power.

The handler should know the basic codes or phrases used by the law enforcement agencies in the area. When working with an agency for the first time, a handler may want to review their basic codes/phrases prior to departing base operations. In the event the agency uses codes instead of phrases, the handler should ask the agency to provide pertinent codes and their meanings in written form. One of the most important codes to know is that which indicates the subject has been located deceased. Should the handler need to contact Command to report this situation, (s)he should follow briefed procedures and wait for clearance before proceeding with the information. This allows Command to ensure all family and press are not in a position to hear further radio communications out of respect for both the deceased and the family.

As previously stated, after locating a deceased subject, the handler should back out of the area and close it off to all parties until a representative from the requesting law enforcement agency arrives to take over the investigation. Under no circumstances should the handler move the body. One should assume that the case has changed from a missing person to a possible homicide investigation, and protect the scene from disturbance until arrival of the appropriate law enforcement personnel. It is not the job of the handler to determine whether or not the subject died as the result of an accident or foul play.

The agency in charge at the scene should handle outside communications, including public relations. Should the press ask a handler for an interview, the handler should refer the request to the agency in charge. Let the agency decide whether or not the handler should be interviewed. If the agency agrees to the interview, the handler should clear with the agency what information should and should not be provided to the press. Once the interview begins, the handler should confine answers to what the agency determined appropriate. This may include what his or her particular canine did in the field.

III. Terminology

The following is a listing of terms and acronyms most commonly used in search and rescue operations.

- RA   Responsible Agency (agency in charge of the scene)

- IC   Incident Commander (person in charge of entire search scene)

- LPQ   Lost person questionnaire (form used to gather info about the missing subject)

- PLS   Point last seen (place subject was last *seen*)

- LKP   Last known point (place subject was *known* to be last)

- DES   Department of Emergency Services [alternately DEM (Division/Department of Emergency Management; OEM (Office of Emergency Management); EMA (Emergency Management Agency) CD (Civil Defense)]

- CISD   Critical incident stress debriefing (program to help those responding to a major incident deal with their feelings and thoughts) [alternately CISM (Critical incident stress management)]

- POD   Probability of detection (probability of finding the subject or clues in the specific area or place)

- ICS   Incident Command System (management structure commonly implemented in many emergency or disaster situations)

41

- Search strategy: A plan or objective to cover a specific area

- Search tactics: Implementation of the strategy

- Walkaway: Person with some mental or cognitive deficiency who has wandered away from a care facility

- Pre-plan: A document, which provides incident managers with information, instructions, resource lists, checklists, Standard Operating Procedures, and technical data that will be used during a search incident.

IV. Lost Person Behavior

Upon arriving at a scene, the handler should obtain as much information as possible about the incident and the missing subject(s), in order to assess the likely behavior of the subject, and decide how best to proceed with the search. The Lost Person Questionnaire (LPQ) provides a predetermined set of questions to ask of the requesting agency. The questionnaire covers such things as the subject's physical description, circumstance of the disappearance, and the health and mental status of the subject.

According to William Syrotuck, the five basic fears of a lost person are: being alone, darkness, animals, suffering and death. Children between the ages of 1-3 years of age and despondent individuals will not generally realize that they are lost, and so by definition do not experience those five basic fears. In most cases, the subject will tend to literally take the path of least resistance. (An exception is the Alzheimer's patient, who will tend to walk until restrained by some object).

A despondent/suicidal person is likely to be found near his or her home, in a scenic area, on high ground or at a location that has special meaning to him or her. When working this type of scene, it is advantageous for the handler to determine where the subject tends to go when upset and how mobile the subject may be.

V. Candidate Study Guide – Lesson Seven (See Attachment I for Answers)

Take a few moments to complete the questions to identify where additional study may be necessary.

1. Regardless of direction, lost persons usually:
   a. Go downhill
   b. Seek paths of least resistance
   c. Go to high ground

2. IC stands for:
   a. Incident Control
   b. Incident Captain
   c. Incident Commander
   d. Instructional Command

3. Children 1-3 years old always know when they are lost.
   a. True
   b. False

4. The handler should not worry if their backups/flankers/walkers become separated from them in the field.
   a. True
   b. False

5. LKP stands for:
   a. Last Known Person
   b. Last Known Point
   c. Last K-9 Point
   d. Local K-9 Police

6. When a deceased subject is found you should NOT:
   a. Move the body
   b. Back away from the body
   c. Report anything that you or the canine may have disturbed
   d. Check for identification of subject

7. LPQ stands for:
   a. Last Person Questioned
   b. Lost Person Questionnaire
   c. Lost Person Question
   d. Last Person Questionnaire

8. A despondent/suicidal person is likely to be found near
    a. His or her home
    b. A Scenic Area
    c. A location that means something to them
    d. All of the above
    e. None of the above

9. Handlers should know basic law enforcement codes prior to departing from base camp to begin searching.
    a. True
    b. False

10. It is the job of the handler to do everything possible to position themselves in front of the press and cameras.
    a. True
    b. False

11. RA stands for
    a. Reasonable Access
    b. Rain Area
    c. Responsible Agency
    d. Reference Azimuth

References

Bryson, S. (1991). *Search Dog Training.* The Boxwood Press, pp. 68-94.

Syrotuck, W. G. (1972). *Scent and the Scenting Dog.* Arner Publications, Inc., pp. 1-81.

"Definitions of Good Samaritan Law on the Web." (2005). Retrieved 05/09/05 from: http://www.google.com/search?hl=en&lr=&ie=UTF-8&oi=defmore&q=define:Good+Samaritan+law.

Recommended Reading

Pearsall, M. D. & Verbruggen, H. MD. (1982). *Scent Training to Track, Search, and Rescue.* Alpine Publications, Inc., pp. 1-44.

Bulanda, S. (1994). *Ready! The Training of the Search and Rescue Dog.* Doral Publishing, pp. 30-36.

Attachment I – Answers to Candidate Study Guide Questions

Lesson One: 1. b, 2. a, 3. d, 4. b, 5. Fracture, 6. Femoral Artery, 7. c, 8. a, 9. a, 10. f, 11. Sprain, 12. Strain, 13. Shock, 14. a, 15. b and d, 16. d

Lesson Two: 1. b, 2. a, 3. b, 4. a, 5. c, 6. b

Lesson Three: 1. b, 2. b, 3. c, 4. b, 5. b, 6. d, 7. d, 8. d

Lesson Four: 1. Airborne rafts and physical disturbance of the earth, 2. a, 3. a, 4. a, 5. a, 6. a, 7. b, 8. d, 9. c, 10. c, 11. e, 12. d, 13. d, 14. a, 15. a, 16. Trailing, 17. Tracking

Lesson Five: 1. a, 2. a, 3. d, 4. b, 5. a, 6. a, 7. b

Lesson Six: 1. c, 2. a, 3. a, 4. b, 5. c, 6. a, 7. Up, 8. Down, 9. a, 10. c, 11., b, 12. b

Lesson Seven: 1. b, 2. c, 3. b, 4. b, 5. b, 6. a, 7. b, 8. d, 9. a, 10. b, 11. c

Attachment II - Scent Pattern Illustrations

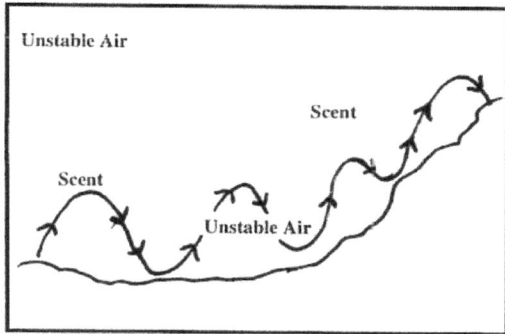

Looping

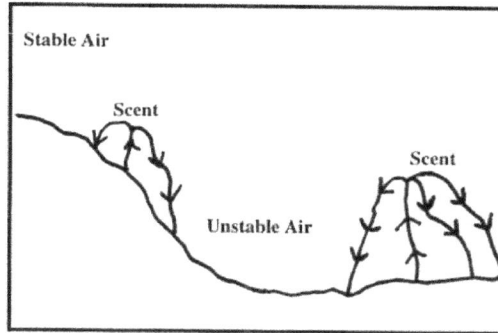

Fumigating(Occurs at Sunrise)

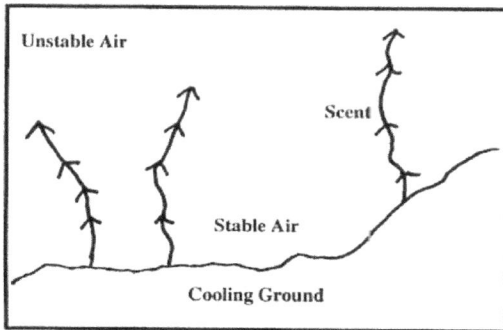

Lofting (Occurs After Sunset)

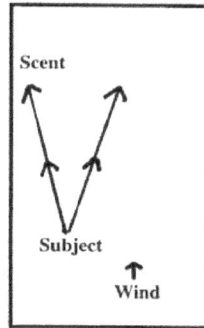

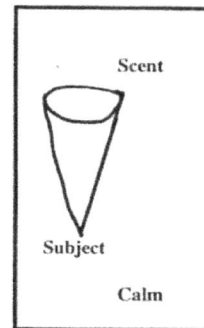

Coning

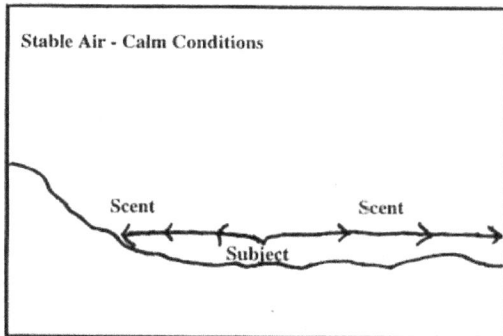

Fanning (Just Before Sunrise)

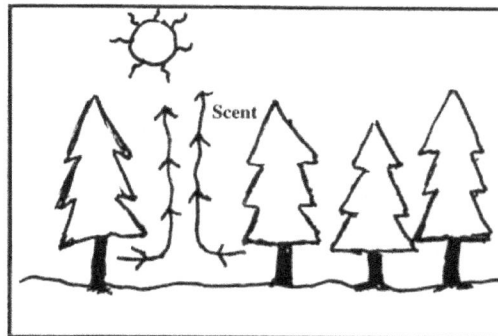

Chimney Effect

www.ingramcontent.com/pod-product-compliance
Lightning Source LLC
Chambersburg PA
CBHW081204270326
41930CB00014B/3300